RyanLindseyFitness
Be so good they can't ignore you

QUICK, EASY, TASTY FAT LOSS RECIPES

Medical Disclaimer

The recipes within these pages are for information purposes only and in no way supersede any prior advice given by a medical practitioner, registered dietician or nutritionist. Should you cook and consume these recipes, you are choosing to do so of your own free will, without coercion and in the full knowledge that the recipes have not been personally designed for you and that should you suffer from a medical condition of any kind or suspect that the ingredients may cause you a medical problem of any kind whatsoever that you should speak to a qualified medical practitioner for advice.

Further, if you choose to cook and consume these recipes and feel that you are experiencing any adverse effects, then you should cease using these recipes immediately and consult your doctor.

Happy Eating! :) Ryan Lindsey

© Copyright 2015 Ryan Lindsey Fitness

All rights reserved.
No part of this book may be reproduced, stored in a retrieval system or transmitted in any form or means whatsoever without the prior consent and written permission of the author.

Contents

Introduction

Smoothies

Mango, mint & cucumber smoothie	1
Alkalising tonic	2
Supreme green smoothie	2
Refresher cooler	3
Pina colada	3
Beetroot, orange & carrot cooler	4
Oaty berry smoothie	5

Snacks

Refreshing cucumber salad	6
Blueberry crunch	7
Banana yoghurt	7

Treats

Flaxseed spelt bread	8
Banana-berry freeze	9
Protein heaven bars	10
Berry sandwich bars	11
Chocolate & coconut bark	12
Carrot & ginger loaf	13
Chocolate nut pancakes	14
Cherry almond muffin loaf	15
Protein jelly	16
Blueberry bombs	17
Sticky popcorn	18
Chocolate nut icecream	19

Breakfast

Crunchy cottage cheese	20
Crunchy quinoa	20
Spiced apple power porridge	21
Bacon & egg frittata	22
Breakfast burrito	23
Summer fruit pancakes	24
Fruit & nut porridge	25
Egg in a cup	26
Thai coconut quiche	27
Piled-high protein brekkie	28
Allowable English brekkie	29
Tasty veg pizza	30
Poached salmon protein brunch	31

Lunch

B.C.T.A.	32
Lentil, sweet potato & coriander stew	33
O-mega salad	34
Egg drop soup	35
Coconut stew	36
Dill & caper salmon burgers	37
Cauliflower chicken	38
Zingy turkey kebabs	39
Sesame chicken	40
Chicken meatballs	41
Fiery fries	42
Salmon asparagus	43
Steak strip salad	44
Tuna & sweet potato crunchy salad	45
Lentil pepper soup	46
Egg & ham salad	47
Hambled eggs	48
Mackerel salad	49
Tomato & basil soup	50
Protein rich omelette	51
5 veg omelette	52
Quick, easy, tasty soup	53

Dinner

Buzzing curry	54
Mediterranean salmon	55
Chicken, rice & pepper pot	56
Warming stew	57
Authentic curry	58
Spaghetti courgetti	59
Lentil & sweet potato curry	60
Chickpea stew	61
Chicken nuggets	62
Chilli con cauli	63
Fragrant fish stir fry	64
Quick fish stew	65
Thai red curry	66
Sizzle steak	67
Cheating stir fry	68
Hot Thai pie	69
Spinach & ricotta pizza	70
Mediterranean chicken	71
Mince masala	72
Fragrant mince	73
Spicy yam soup	74
Spicy Thai burgers	75
Satay spice kebabs	76
Lime chicken fajitas	77

Welcome

Welcome to the Quick, Easy, Tasty Fat Loss Recipes Book. This book will be your bible over the coming weeks! In case you didn't know, nutrition will count for about 80% of your results. That's right 80%! There is an important lesson to be learned from the story below...

You see I used to have a client, let's call her Lisa. Now Lisa trained very hard and never missed a training session and so with all this effort and dedication to her training she thought that the scales and the measuring tape would really be moving in the right direction at her weights and measurement day.

I will never forget the look on her face when she found out that she lost only 1lb and half an inch from her waist. She was disappointed and so was I.

"You have read the information on the importance of nutrition and you have been using the recipe book I gave you?," I asked. It turned out she never read it because she thought she already knew about nutrition and that her personal trainer wasn't going to know more than she did.

Sometimes we learn the hard way! I'm pleased to say that once Lisa had become fully aware of the importance of nutrition for fat loss, we were able to make some important changes. 28 days later she was 14lbs down and almost 2 dress sizes smaller.

As the saying goes,

"When the student is ready, the teacher will appear."

And you are ready! That's why you are reading this!

Below I have included the key principles that work for nutrition for health and fat loss. If anything you read, see or hear deviates from any of the six principles below, chances are you can dismiss it immediately as a short term fad diet. This is a way of eating that will enable you to achieve both fast and permanent results in a way that is 100% sustainable. You see this change has to be permanent so it has to be both straightforward and above all enjoyable. The good news is that my recipe book will show you how quick, easy and tasty eating this way is.

Follow these principles and you will get results...

1. Eating fewer calories than you burn (calorie deficit)
2. Eat more vegetables and fruits because they are rich in antioxidants and micro-nutrients (vitamins and minerals)
3. Eat plenty of protein for repair and maintenance of lean tissue, and to keep you feeling full (protein satisfies the appetite more than any other macronutrient)
4. Eat enough healthy fats from oily fish, nuts, avocados, coconut and olive oils (healthy fats are an essential part of a balanced diet)
5. Drink plenty of water to naturally detoxify the body, keeping the brain and body hydrated so it can function properly (green and herbal teas count towards this water intake)
6. Limit processed foods and artificial sweeteners and preservatives

Now go and learn, cook, and experience the benefits that my recipes have to offer – enjoy!

Let's get started...

Below are a few hints and tips to help you along the way. I recommend you spare a few minutes to read this before you get cooking.

COOKING WITH FATS AND OILS

For cooking and frying at high temperatures, **coconut oil** is safe to use, as it remains stable at higher temperatures. In other words, unlike many other oils and fats, it won't become damaged when heated above a certain temperature. When oils become damaged, they turn rancid, which can be damaging to your body. Coconut oil is high in lauric acid, a fatty acid that is anti-fungal, anti-bacterial and anti-viral.

For salads, use cold pressed extra virgin olive oils, sesame or peanut oils. There are also a variety of fats and oils that should be avoided completely. All hydrogenated and partially hydrogenated oils are bad for you and can contribute to a range of serious health problems such as cancer, heart disease and immune dysfunction.

COCONUT FLOUR

A gluten free alternative to normal flour. This is a versatile ingredient, which can be used in baking and cooking. Also makes great pancakes!

WHERE TO BUY

Coconut Oil. Approx. **£9.00** for a **500g pot** on **Amazon**

Coconut Flour. Approx. **£6.75** for a **500g bag** on **Amazon**

Ryan-Lindsey-Fitness | 07547 192913

TEA

Green tea has lots of amazing health benefits. It is high in antioxidants and contains about half the amount of caffeine of normal tea. It is widely available in supermarkets, health shops and online.

Tulsi Brahmi (caffeine free) is another healthy alternative with healing properties, as well as also being a rich source of antioxidants.

Of all herbal teas, licorice tea is arguably one of the most beneficial yet under-appreciated herbal teas. Licorice tea can help the liver to rid the body of unwanted toxins, can relieve constipation, is used to treat low blood pressure, helps to lower cholesterol and is an anti-allergenic so is helpful for hay fever and conjunctivitis sufferers.

STORECUPBOARD SAVIOURS

There are plenty of simple ways to make your food taste good. Why not keep your cupboards stocked up with a handy supply of spices and rubs, which are generally very cheap to buy, simple to use, and a much healthier alternative to the artificial flavourings, additives and sugars found in many of the processed sauces available.

Consider replacing cheap, processed table salt (which is full of chemicals, and some brands even contain sugar!) with a good quality organic sea salt or Himalayan pink salt. This salt contains many beneficial minerals and can help balance electrolytes, eliminate toxins and support nutrient absorption.

WHERE TO BUY

Tulsi Brahmi Tea. Approx. **£1.25** for **25 bags** at **Amazon** and www.discount-supplements.co.uk

Licorice Tea. Approx. **£1.25** for **20 bags** in **major supermarkets**

Himalayan Pink Salt. Approx. **£3.00** for a **140g pot** on **Amazon**

A LITTLE SWEETNESS

Sugar gets a lot of bad press these days due to the negative effects it can have on your health. For example, excessive consumption suppresses the immune system and reduces insulin sensitivity.

However, I believe it is important to consider the for and against, and not just react to what we see in the news. If you lead a healthy lifestyle, eat a balanced, varied diet, and enjoy moderate regular exercise, then there really shouldn't be cause for panic.

Within the huge category that sugar spans, are a range of good and bad food choices. If, for example, you cut out all fruit for the rest of your life (because fruit contains sugar), you might well miss out on some key nutrients. Plus you might feel deprived.

My advice to you is that it is your choice if you consume sugar and/or sugar alternatives. But what is probably more important is to consider that worrying about the matter could be equally bad or even worse for your health. Instead, why not try to look at sugar and sugar alternatives as a 'treat' rather than a necessity... something to really savour and enjoy every once in a while (without the guilt!).

In some of my recipes I have used natural sweeteners such as Stevia. Many research studies have been conducted on the safety of these products and while no definite links have been made to any negative health effects, overall the evidence for and against it is still inconclusive. If you'd prefer to swap the sweeteners in my recipes with something else then feel free to do so. Home made apple sauce, raisins and bananas can add enough sweetness to a variety of baking recipes.

Note: There are several forms of Stevia and available - a very light powdery texture, and a more granulated/grainy texture. In all of my recipes, I have used the granulated version. I recommend you use the same, so that the ingredient weight is accurate.

WHERE TO BUY

Stevia. Approx. **£5.00** for **40 sachet sticks** on **Amazon**

FLAXSEED

Flaxseed is rich in omega-3 fatty acids and fibre. It is a great ingredient to use in cooking and baking, e.g. spelt bread, cakes, pizzas (yes, healthy ones!), mixed in with nut butter or humous dips, added to pancake mixes, sprinkled over cereals or salads or added to smoothies.

It's best to grind the flaxseed up in a coffee grinder first, as it is not absorbed by the body if left whole. If you mix flaxseed with water and leave to stand for 10 minutes, it develops a sticky coating, which makes it a great egg substitute in baking (as do chia seeds). Always store your flaxseed in the fridge in an airtight container.

WHERE TO BUY

Flaxseed. Approx. **£5.20** for a **425g bag** in **major supermarkets**

WHITE OR WHOLEGRAIN RICE?

Generally speaking, wholegrain, unprocessed carbohydrates tend to be better handled than processed carbohydrates such as white rice, pasta, bread and cereals.

Wholegrain rice is probably a healthier option than white rice, nevertheless it should still be consumed in moderation, especially if you are trying to lose fat.

In most cases, where rice appears in this book, I haven't specified white or wholegrain rice. Please decide for yourself which is the best option for you.

A helping hand...

Through a combination of good nutrition and exercise, the following recipes will help you achieve optimum fat loss results.

Here are some low carb recipes, ideal for a NON TRAINING DAY:

Breakfast
- Bacon & Egg Frittata
- Thai Coconut Quiche
- Allowable English Brekkie

Lunch & Dinner
- Dill & Caper Salmon Burgers
- Chicken Meatballs
- Hambled Eggs
- B.C.T. A.
- Mediterranean Chicken
- Protein Rich Omelette
- Lime Chicken Fajitas
- Quick Fish Stew

Snacks & Treats
- Chocolate Nut Pancakes
- Refreshing Cucumber Salad
- Protein Jelly

Smoothies
- Pina Colada

Research has shown that the body can tolerate carbohydrate better after exercise. If you are going to consume carbs, you should aim to do this within 2 hours of exercise.

Here are some recipes which are ideal post-workout.
These are also medium / high protein to aid muscle repair.

Breakfast
- Crunchy Quinoa
- Fruit & Nut Porridge
- Breakfast Burrito

Lunch & Dinner
- Tuna & Sweet Potato Crunchy Salad
- Buzzing Curry
- Chicken, Rice & Pepper Pot
- Authentic Curry
- Chilli Con Cauli
- Fragrant Fish Stir Fry
- Thai Red Curry
- Sizzle Steak
- Spicy Yam Soup

Snacks & Treats
- Flaxseed Spelt Bread
- Carrot & Ginger Loaf
- Banana Yoghurt

Smoothies
- Beetroot, Orange & Carrot Cooler

Mango, mint & cucumber smoothie

200g fresh mango, roughly chopped
100g cucumber
60g fresh spinach
1 tbsp coconut milk (optional)
5 icecubes
100ml cold fresh water
1 sprig fresh mint

SERVES 2

Put all the ingredients into a blender and whizz until smooth. Add more water if necessary to achieve the desired consistency.

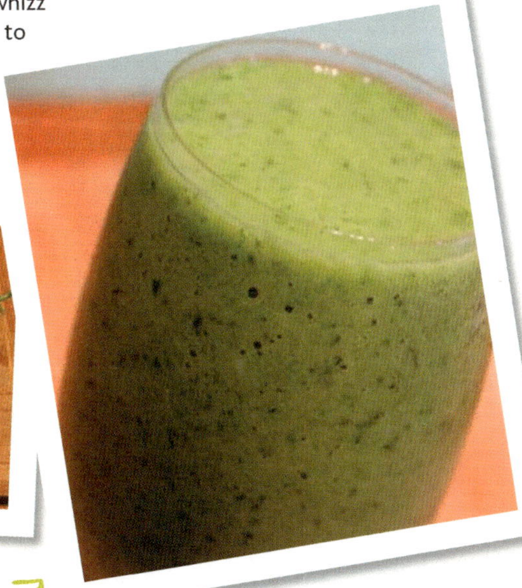

PER SERVING:
81 Calories
16g Carbs
2g Protein
1g Fat

Ryan-Lindsey-Fitness | 07547 192913

Alkalising tonic

handful fresh spinach
1 kiwi, halved
2 tbsps wheatgrass powder
juice of half a lemon
300ml cold water (add more or less, depending on desired consistency)

READY IN 5 MINUTES

Put all the ingredients into a blender and whizz until smooth.

SERVES 1

PER SERVING:
121 Calories
20g Carbs
8g Protein
1g Fat

Supreme green smoothie

30g baby leaf spinach
15g fresh ginger, peeled and roughly chopped
1 tsp wheatgrass powder
50g blueberries
200ml cold water (add more or less, depending on desired consistency)

READY IN 5 MINUTES

Put all the ingredients into a blender and whizz until smooth.

SERVES 1

PER SERVING:
64 Calories
11g Carbs
5g Protein
0g Fat

2 SMOOTHIES

Refresher Cooler

50g fresh mango
handful fresh spinach
1 tbsp wheatgrass powder
handful cucumber, roughly diced
1 kiwi, peeled and diced
handful ice cubes

SERVES 1

Put all the ingredients into a blender and whizz until smooth. Add more water if necessary to achieve the desired consistency.

PER SERVING:
109 Calories
21g Carbs
4g Protein
1g Fat

Pina colada

1 slice fresh pineapple, peeled and chopped roughly
1 tbsp coconut cream
handful ice cubes
40g vanilla flavoured whey protein (optional)

SERVES 2

PER SERVING:
145 Calories
7g Carbs
15g Protein
6g Fat

Put all the ingredients into a blender and whizz until smooth.

Ryan-Lindsey-Fitness | 07547 192913   SMOOTHIES   3

Beetroot, orange & carrot cooler

READY IN 5 MINUTES

2 cooked beetroots
juice of one large orange
3 medium sized carrots, peeled and cut in half
1 tsp chia seeds (optional)
handful ice cubes
150ml cold fresh water

SERVES 2

Put all the ingredients into a blender and whizz until smooth. Add more water if necessary to achieve the desired consistency.

PER SERVING:
97 Calories
19g Carbs
3g Protein
1g Fat

Oaty berry smoothie

25g vanilla or strawberry flavoured whey protein
70g frozen mixed berries
15g porridge oats (use gluten-free oats if preferred)
100ml cold fresh water

SERVES 1

Put the whey protein, berries and oats into a blender and add half of the water.

Blend together, adding more water until you have the desired consistency.

PER SERVING:
145 Calories
14g Carbs
20g Protein
1g Fat

Ryan-Lindsey-Fitness | 07547 192913   SMOOTHIES   5

Refreshing cucumber salad

READY IN 5 MINUTES

1 cucumber, halved lengthways and cut into long strips
1 tbsp olive oil
handful fresh mint, finely chopped
pinch of sea salt

SERVES 2

Prepare a medium grill. Place the cucumber strips onto a baking tray and lightly drizzle with oil.

Grill for 5 minutes until the cucumbers have softened slightly.

Serve with a sprinkle of mint and sea salt.

Suggestion:
Ideal as a quick snack or as an accompaniment to lunch or dinner

PER SERVING:
75 Calories
2g Carbs
1g Protein
7g Fat

Blueberry crunch

100g low fat Greek yoghurt (use dairy free yoghurt if preferred)
50g fresh blueberries
15g chopped hazelnuts

SERVES 1

READY IN 5 MINUTES

Place the yoghurt into a bowl.
Top with the blueberries and hazelnuts.

PER SERVING:
205 Calories
16g Carbs
6g Protein
13g Fat

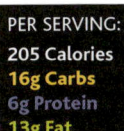

Banana yoghurt

60g low fat Greek yoghurt (use dairy free yoghurt if preferred)
1 medium sized banana, chopped
15g flaked almonds
1 tsp acacia honey

SERVES 1

READY IN 5 MINUTES

Place the yoghurt into a bowl.
Top with the banana, almonds and honey.

PER SERVING:
242 Calories
32g Carbs
6g Protein
10g Fat

Ryan-Lindsey-Fitness | 07547 192913   SNACKS

Flaxseed spelt bread

500g wholegrain spelt flour
(use gluten free flour if preferred)
½ tsp salt
1 tsp quick yeast
3 tbsps flaxseed
400ml warm water
1 tbsp olive oil

SERVES 6

Preheat oven to 200°C. Line the base of two medium sized bread tins with baking paper.

In a large bowl, mix together the flour, salt, flaxseed and yeast.

Roughly mix the water into the flour. While the dough is still craggy, add the olive oil and give it a good mix.

Knead the dough for several minutes, using a little extra flour to stop it sticking to your hands.

Divide the mixture into the two bread tins. Cover with a clean tea towel, and leave somewhere warm for 25 minutes e.g. next to a radiator.

Bake for 40-45 minutes. Turn out the loaves onto a wire rack and allow to cool for at least 5 minutes before serving.

Recommended:
Flaxseed is a great antioxidant, rich in Omega 3 essential fatty acids and fibre

PER SERVING:
331 Calories
54g Carbs
13g Protein
7g Fat

Banana-berry freeze

1 banana
300g frozen raspberries
100g low fat Greek yoghurt (use dairy free yoghurt if preferred)
1 tbsp acacia honey
1 sheet baking paper

SERVES 4

Cut the banana into thin slices, and place on a lined tray. Freeze for one hour.

Remove bananas from the freezer and place in a food processor with the frozen raspberries.

Leave for 10 minutes to soften up. Add honey and yoghurt and pulse until creamy. If the processor gets stuck, wait a few minutes for the mixture to soften up before continuing.

Serve immediately or freeze for a later date. Remove from the freezer 15 minutes before serving.

Top Tip:
A healthy dessert packed full of antioxidants, ideal for entertaining guests

PER SERVING:
109 Calories
21g Carbs
4g Protein
1g Fat

 Ryan-Lindsey-Fitness | 07547 192913   TREATS

Protein heaven bars
(like snickers in disguise)

3 medium sized bananas
50g crunchy peanut butter (no added sugar)
2 medium sized eggs
1 egg white
40g porridge oats (use gluten free oats if preferred)
20g ground almonds
30g flaxseed, whole or ground
50g chocolate flavoured whey protein
30g organic raisins
20g dark chocolate (minimum 70% cocoa), finely chopped

MAKES 9 BARS

Preheat oven to 190°C.

Line a baking tray with parchment paper.

In a large bowl, mash the bananas. Add all of the other ingredients and mix thoroughly. Pour the mixture onto the tray and flatten with a spoon.

Bake in the oven for 15 minutes.

Allow to cool on a rack, then chop into nine pieces.

Store in an airtight container for up to four days.

Top Tip:
200g blueberries will work as an alternative to the banana. It also reduces the carbs.

PER SERVING: with banana / blueberries
169 Calories / 160 Calories
13g Carbs / 11g Carbs
11g Protein / 11g Protein
8g Fat / 8g Fat

TREATS

Berry sandwich bars

100g coconut flour
60g vanilla flavoured whey protein (optional)
1 tbsp ground flaxseed
½ tsp baking soda
1½ tsps cinnamon
½ tsp sea salt
50ml organic coconut oil
25ml light unsweetened coconut milk
4 medium sized eggs
2 tsp vanilla extract
20g pitted dates, finely chopped
200g mixed berries
10g unsweetened coconut flakes

MAKES 8 SQUARES

Preheat the oven to 175°C. Line a 9x9 inch baking tray with greaseproof paper.

Sieve the flour into a bowl and add the whey protein (if using), flaxseed, baking soda, cinnamon, and salt. Set aside.

In a separate bowl whisk together the coconut oil, coconut milk, eggs, and vanilla until creamy. Add the dates then slowly stir in the flour mixture until well combined and a firm dough forms.

PER SQUARE:
204 Calories
12g Carbs
12g Protein
12g Fat

Divide the dough in half and press half evenly into the bottom of the parchment lined pan. Spread the berries evenly over top of the dough.

On a separate sheet of greaseproof paper, gently shape the remaining dough into a similar size and shape as before. Lift the dough onto the paper and transfer over the berries like a lid, removing the paper as you go. If it breaks apart, that's fine, just cover the berries as much as possible. Sprinkle the dough lid with coconut flakes, and press lightly to hold them in place.

Bake for 20 minutes, until the coconut is golden and they spring back to the touch. Allow to cool in the pan completely before cutting into squares. Store in an airtight container and refrigerate for up to 4 days.

Ryan-Lindsey-Fitness | 07547 192913

TREATS

Chocolate & coconut bark

80g organic coconut oil
3 tbsps organic cocoa powder
1 tsp stevia or xylitol
80g chopped nuts
50g chocolate flavoured whey protein (optional)

SERVES 6

RyanLindseyFitness
Be so good they can't ignore you

A low carb treat that tastes truly indulgent and will satisfy any sweet tooth.

You can use any type of nuts. Hazelnuts, brazils, macademias or pistachios work very well. Chop them roughly to add extra texture.

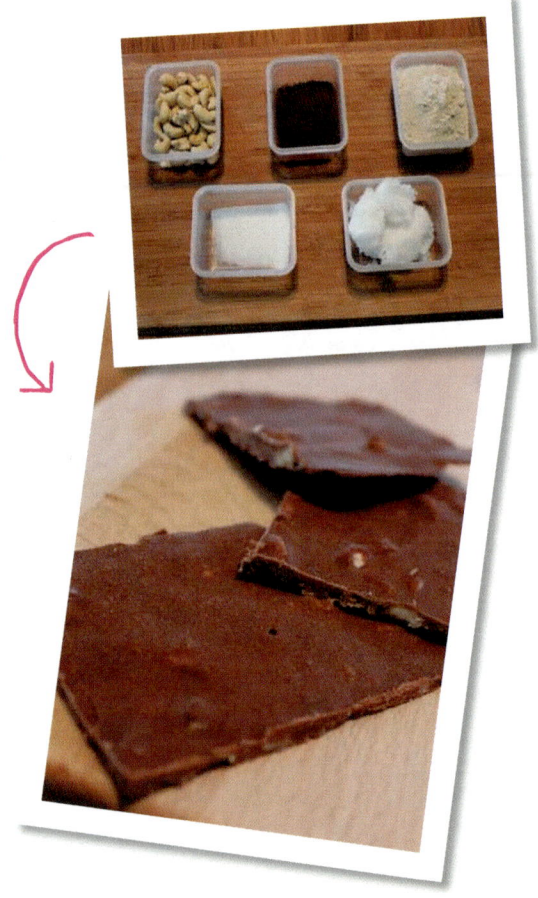

Line a baking tray with greaseproof paper and put in the freezer.

Melt the coconut oil gently in a pan over a medium/low heat. Add the cocoa powder and stevia/xylitol. Stir well to combine. Remove from heat.

Stir the nuts and whey protein into the mixture. Add a little cold water so that the consistency is thick but pourable.

Remove baking tray from freezer and pour the mixture onto the baking paper, spreading evenly to desired thickness.

Put in freezer on a level shelf and leave for 20 minutes. Freeze for up to 2 weeks.

PER SERVING:
222 Calories
3g Carbs
9g Protein
22g Fat

Carrot & ginger loaf

20g flaxseed, ground
180g bramley apple, peeled, cored and sliced
150g coconut flour
½ tsp xanthan gum
2 tsps baking powder
50g chocolate flavour whey protein (optional)
pinch of sea salt
2 tsps ground cinnamon
1 tsp ground ginger
8 cloves, ground
3 tsps stevia/xylitol
50g coconut palm sugar
100ml light coconut milk
100ml extra virgin olive oil
1 egg
1 egg white
200g carrots, peeled and grated
80g organic raisins
20g nuts, chopped (any kind)

MAKES 14 SLICES

Preheat oven to 180°C. Line the base of two medium sized loaf tins with greaseproof paper.

Mix the flaxseed with a little water until the consistency thickens. Leave to stand.

Bring a small saucepan of water to the boil. Add the apple and simmer gently for around 4 minutes, until soft. Remove from heat and drain through a fine sieve. Stir gently to remove excess water. Transfer apple to a bowl and leave to cool.

In a large bowl, mix the flour, xanthan gum, baking powder, whey protein (if using), salt, cinnamon, ginger, cloves, stevia/xylitol and coconut sugar.

In a separate bowl, mix the coconut milk, olive oil, egg, egg white, apple sauce until smooth. Gently stir in the carrots and raisins and mix.

Divide the mixture between the two loaf tins and sprinkle the nuts over the top.

Bake for 30 minutes. Remove from oven and leave to cool for 5 minutes on a wire rack. Remove from tins and allow to cool. Store in an airtight container for up to 3 days.

PER SLICE:
191 Calories
15g Carbs
8g Protein
11g Fat

Ryan-Lindsey-Fitness | 07547 192913

TREATS

Chocolate nut pancakes

25g coconut flour
25g chocolate flavour whey protein
30g whole porridge oats (use gluten free oats if preferred)
2 medium sized eggs
1 egg white
1 tsp cocoa powder
1 tsp stevia/xylitol
20g dark chocolate (minimum 70% cocoa)
15g crunchy peanut butter (no added sugar)
10g organic coconut oil

MAKES 5 PANCAKES

Put all of the ingredients except for the oil into a blender and mix together. Add a little water if necessary to achieve the right consistency. The mixture should be quite thick yet runny enough to pour.

Heat some of the coconut oil in a large non stick pan over a medium/high heat. Pour one quarter of the mixture into the centre of the pan. Move the pan around gently to even out the mixture into a circular shape.

When small holes appear in the pancake, turn or flip it over and heat on the other side for 1-2 minutes.

Transfer pancake to a plate. Add more oil to the pan and repeat the process with the remaining batter.

These can be kept in the refrigerator for up to 2 days.

PER PANCAKE:
148 Calories
9g Carbs
10g Protein
8g Fat

Serving suggestion:

Serve with a dollop of Greek yoghurt, black cherries (fresh or frozen) and some grated dark chocolate.

14 TREATS

Cherry almond muffin loaf

50g bramley apple, cored, peeled and sliced
5 medium sized eggs
1 egg white
30g pitted dark cherries, halved
80g coconut flour
65g agave syrup
1½ tsps stevia/xylitol
70g ground almonds
1 tsp of vanilla essence
1 tsp bicarbonate of soda

MAKES 10 SLICES

Healthy baking - fun for the family!

Preheat oven to 180°C.

Line the base of a medium sized loaf tin with greaseproof paper.

Bring a small saucepan of water to the boil. Add the apple and simmer gently for around 4 minutes, until soft. Remove from heat and drain through a fine sieve. Stir gently to remove excess water. Transfer apple to a bowl and leave to cool.

Beat the eggs and egg whites with a whisk for 30 seconds.

Add all of the remaining ingredients and mix well. Pour the mixture into the loaf tin and bake for 40-50 minutes, until golden brown.

Leave to cool for 5 minutes, then remove from the tin and transfer to a wire rack to cool.

PER SLICE:
132 Calories
12g Carbs
7g Protein
7g Fat

Ryan-Lindsey-Fitness | 07547 192913   TREATS

Protein jelly

1 sachet/pack sugar free strawberry or raspberry jelly* (use a vegetarian jelly if preferred)
½ pint of boiling water
40g strawberry flavoured whey protein powder
½ pint of cold water
50g berries

SERVES 3

If possible, use jelly which is free from artificial sweeteners, flavours, and colourings

Add the jelly to the boiling water. Stir well until the jelly has dissolved.

Stir in the whey protein. Top up with cold water.

Pour into dessert bowls or glasses and add the berries.

Refrigerate until set.

Store in the refrigerator for up to 3 days.

PER SERVING:
60 Calories
2g Carbs
13g Protein
0g Fat

Blueberry bombs

2 tbsps dark chocolate (minimum 70% cocoa)
1 tsp vanilla extract
3 tbsps acacia honey
4 tbsps crunchy peanut butter (no added sugar)
100g porridge oats (use gluten free oats if preferred)
50ml light unsweetened coconut milk
3 tbsps omega sprinkle (flaxseed, linseed, sesame seeds, sunflower seeds)
80g pitted prunes
2 tbsps organic desiccated coconut
75g blueberries

MAKES 15 SERVINGS

Put the chocolate in a heatproof bowl. Pour several inches of boiling water into a shallow wide based dish. Place over a gentle heat and allow the water to simmer gently.

Carefully sit the heatproof bowl in the shallow dish of water. Melt the chocolate slowly, stirring regularly. Remove from heat.

Add the remaining ingredients and mix well.

Refrigerate for several hours.

Roll into 15 balls. Refrigerate until ready to serve.

Store in an airtight container and refrigerate for up to 4 days.

PER SERVING:
136 Calories
12g Carbs
4g Protein
8g Fat

Ryan-Lindsey-Fitness | 07547 192913   TREATS

Sticky popcorn

80g popping corn
15g organic coconut oil
15g coconut sugar

SERVES 4

Melt the oil over a medium/high heat in a large saucepan.

Add the popping corn and cover.

When the corn starts to pop, shake the pan gently from time to time over the heat, to prevent burning.

When most of the corn has popped remove saucepan from heat. You will probably find there are a few that remain unpopped.

Transfer to a large serving bowl.

Sprinkle on the coconut sugar and mix well.

The sugar will melt slightly onto the warm popcorn to give a slightly sticky coating.

Warning: Leave a few minutes to cool before eating as warm sugar can burn.

PER SERVING
145 Calories
14g Carbs
2g Protein
9g Fat

Chocolate nut icecream

500g 0% fat Greek yoghurt (use dairy free yoghurt if preferred)
2 medium sized ripe bananas, sliced
50g chocolate flavour whey protein
1 tsp vanilla essence
10g dark chocolate (minimum 70% cocoa), finely chopped
20g chopped hazelnuts

SERVES 6

Put the yoghurt, banana, whey protein and vanilla essence in a blender. Pulse until creamy.

Stir in the dark chocolate and nuts.

Divide into 6 small freezer proof pots

Freeze for at least 2 hours. Remove from freezer 15 minutes before serving.

PER SERVING
156 Calories
14g Carbs
16g Protein
4g Fat

Ryan-Lindsey-Fitness | 07547 192913

TREATS

Crunchy cottage cheese

175g cottage cheese
1 kiwi diced
15g flaked almonds

SERVES 1

Put the cottage cheese in a bowl, and top with the kiwis and almonds.

PER SERVING:
288 Calories
21g Carbs
24g Protein
12g Fat

Crunchy quinoa

60g uncooked quinoa
50g low fat Greek yoghurt (use dairy free yoghurt if preferred)
20g dried pitted prunes
15g flaked almonds
½ tsp ground cinnamon

SERVES 1

Cook the quinoa according to packet instructions. You might prefer to do this the night before to save time in the morning. Cool the quinoa with cold spring water.

Drain and serve in a bowl topped with yoghurt, almonds, prunes and a sprinkle of cinnamon.

PER SERVING:
379 Calories
53g Carbs
17g Protein
11g Fat

Spiced apple power porridge

40g porridge oats, (use gluten free oats if preferred) soaked overnight in cold fresh water
1 medium sized apple, diced
15g flaxseed, ground
1 tsp ground cinnamon

SERVES 1

Place the soaked oats into a saucepan and cook over a medium heat for several minutes, stirring continuously.

Add the diced apple and cook for several minutes. Stir in the flaxseed.

Spoon the contents into a bowl, and sprinkle with cinnamon.

Top Tip:

Soaking the oats for at least 12 hours overnight makes it much easier for the body to digest.

This also speeds up the cooking process, which is ideal if you are short on time in the mornings

PER SERVING:
241 Calories
44g Carbs
5g Protein
5g Fat

Ryan-Lindsey-Fitness | 07547 192913

Bacon & egg frittata

3 medium sized eggs, yolks and whites separated
1 tsp organic butter
2 rashers unsmoked back bacon, diced (use a vegetarian bacon* if preferred)
sprinkle parsley

SERVES 1

Suggestion:

Try to use unprocessed bacon, preferably cured with natural ingredients, that contains no added artificial ingredients or preservatives. Try your local butcher or farm shop

** **Note:** Some meat free alternatives contain gluten and/or MSG. Please check the label before you buy!*

Preheat oven to 175°C.

Beat the egg whites in a bowl, until stiff peaks form.

In a separate bowl, beat the yolks and half of the butter together.

Gently melt the remaining butter in a pan and gently fry the bacon for around 5 minutes. Remove from pan.

Gently fold the egg yolks and bacon into the egg whites.

Pour the batter back into the skillet so that it covers the base of the pan evenly. Cook on a medium heat for two minutes, then bake in the oven for 15 minutes.

Remove the soufflé gently from the skillet, loosening with a spatula.

Garnish with a sprinkle of parsley.

PER SERVING:
396 Calories
0g Carbs
27g Protein
32g Fat

Breakfast burrito

READY IN 10 MINUTES

3 medium sized eggs, yolks and whites separated
5g organic coconut oil
half a small red onion, finely chopped
1 tomato, finely chopped
1 green chilli, finely chopped
½ yellow or red pepper, diced
handful fresh coriander, finely chopped
60g cooked chicken/Quorn meat free chicken*
¼ avocado, cut into small chunks

SERVES 1

*** Note:** *Some meat free alternatives contain gluten and/or MSG. Please check the label before you buy!*

Whisk the egg whites.

Melt half of the coconut oil in a lightly warmed skillet. Pour half the egg whites into the pan, swirling to spread them evenly. After 30 seconds, cover and cook for 1 minute. Use a spatula to loosen and slide onto a plate. Repeat this process with remaining egg whites.

PER SERVING:
540 Calories
20g Carbs
43g Protein
32g Fat

Sauté the onion with the remaining oil for one minute then add tomato, chillis, pepper, coriander and chicken. Whisk egg yolks and pour into the pan, mixing well into the other ingredients.

Add the avocado then spoon half of the filling onto each egg white. Roll the egg white up into burritos.

A perfect weekend treat!

Ryan-Lindsey-Fitness | 07547 192913 — BREAKFAST — 23

Summer fruit pancakes

3 tsps coconut flour
2 medium sized eggs
½ tsp ground cinnamon
2 tsps stevia/xylitol
1 tsp organic coconut oil
1 tbsp low fat Greek yoghurt (use dairy free yoghurt if preferred)
100g mixed berries and fruit, chopped into small pieces

SERVES 1

Suggestion:

Choose low/medium-sugar fruits, such as blueberries, kiwis and strawberries, rather than high-sugar fruits, such as bananas, apples and mangos if you are limiting your carb intake

Place the flour, eggs, cinnamon and stevia/xylitol in a blender and mix until smooth. Add more flour if necessary to achieve a medium consistency (pourable but not runny).

Heat the coconut oil in a pan to a medium/high heat and then pour in a small amount of the mixture into the centre of the pan (around 50ml).

Move the pan around gently to even out the mixture into a circular shape. When small holes appear in the pancake, turn it over and heat on the other side for 1-2 minutes. Repeat with the remaining batter.

Serve with yoghurt and fruit.

PER SERVING:
339 Calories
14g Carbs
19g Protein
23g Fat

24 BREAKFAST

Fruit & nut porridge

40g porridge oats, (use gluten free oats if preferred) soaked overnight in cold fresh water
1 tsp stevia/xylitol
1 kiwi, diced
15g flaked almonds
handful dried prunes, chopped

SERVES 1

Top Tip:

Soaking the oats overnight – for at least 12 hours – makes it much easier for the body to digest.

This also speeds up the cooking process – ideal if you are short on time in the mornings

Place the soaked oats into a saucepan and cook over a medium heat for several minutes, stirring continuously. Stir in the stevia/xylitol.

Spoon the contents into a bowl. Add the kiwi, almonds, and prunes.

PER SERVING:
340 Calories
48g Carbs
10g Protein
12g Fat

Ryan-Lindsey-Fitness | 07547 192913

BREAKFAST

Egg in a cup

2 medium sized eggs
2 oatcakes
5g organic butter
salt and pepper

SERVES 1

Boil the eggs in a pan of salted water for 10 minutes. Place in cold water for one minute to cool, then peel.

Place in a cup with butter and season with salt and pepper. Mash thoroughly with a fork.

Spread thickly onto oatcakes.

PER SERVING:
283 Calories
12g Carbs
16g Protein
19g Fat

Thai coconut quiche

10g organic coconut oil, for greasing
handful of broccoli, chopped into medium sized pieces
6 medium sized eggs
2 salad tomatoes
2 shallots
1 garlic clove
1 stick lemongrass
400ml light unsweetened coconut milk
½ tsp chilli flakes

SERVES 4

Preheat oven to 200°C.

Grease a 10-inch round or 13x9 inch square baking dish. Cook the broccoli in boiling water for 4 minutes, then drain.

In a blender, mix together the remaining ingredients. Stir in the broccoli.

Pour the mixture in a baking dish and bake in the oven for 20 minutes or until set in the middle.

PER SERVING:
232 Calories
9g Carbs
13g Protein
16g Fat

Ryan-Lindsey-Fitness | 07547 192913

BREAKFAST

Piled-high protein brekkie

2 medium sized eggs
large handful of spinach
15g plain cashews
½ tsp salad seasoning (recipe below)

SERVES 1

Easy to make salad seasoning:
Lemongrass, Coriander & Garlic

In a grinder, mix up a teaspoon of the following: Dried lemongrass, ground coriander and garlic powder. Add a good pinch of rock salt. Adjust quantities to taste. Store in an airtight container for future use.

PER SERVING:
289 Calories
6g Carbs
19g Protein
21g Fat

Boil the eggs in a pan of salted water for 10 minutes.

While they are cooking, steam the spinach gently for 3-4 minutes, until wilted.

Remove the eggs from the heat, and cool down for one minute with cold water, before peeling.

Serve the eggs sliced over a bed of spinach. Add the cashew nuts and sprinkle with seasoning.

BREAKFAST

Allowable English brekkie

10g organic coconut oil
4 rashers unsmoked bacon (use a vegetarian bacon* if preferred)
handful closed cup mushrooms, chopped
2 tomatoes, halved
4 medium sized eggs

SERVES 2

Suggestion:

Try to use unprocessed bacon, preferably cured with natural ingredients, that contains no added artificial ingredients or preservatives. Try your local butcher or farm shop

In a pan, heat the coconut oil to a medium/high heat. Fry the bacon rashers on both sides until crispy. Add the mushrooms and fry for several minutes. Remove from pan.

Next, fry the tomatoes gently for several minutes on each side. Remove pan from the heat.

Break the eggs into a jug and whisk gently. Cook the eggs over a medium heat in a saucepan, stirring all the time. When the eggs are cooked, remove from heat, and transfer to a plate with the bacon, mushrooms and tomatoes.

* *Note: Some meat free alternatives contain gluten and/or MSG. Please check the label before you buy!*

PER SERVING:
417 Calories
6g Carbs
33g Protein
29g Fat

Ryan-Lindsey-Fitness | 07547 192913

Tasty veg pizza

4 medium sized eggs
3 egg whites
Himalayan pink salt to season
40g porridge oats (use gluten free oats if preferred)
7 cherry tomatoes, halved
60g baby leaf spinach, finely chopped
1 green chilli pepper, finely chopped
½ a large green pepper, finely chopped
1 tsp paprika
½ tsp dried oregano
15g low fat cheddar cheese, grated (use a dairy free cheese if preferred)

MAKES 8 SLICES

Top tip:
This pizza makes a great portable snack

Preheat oven to 150°C.

Lightly grease a large round ovenproof dish with coconut oil or butter.

Whisk the eggs and egg whites in a jug and season well with Himalayan salt. Add the oats, vegetables, dried spices and herbs. Stir well. Pour into the dish and cook for 10 minutes.

Remove from oven and sprinkle on the cheese.

Cook for a further 5 minutes, or until centre of pizza is cooked.

Refrigerate any leftovers for up to 3 days.

PER SLICE:
63 Calories
4g Carbs
6g Protein
3g Fat

30 BREAKFAST

Poached salmon protein brunch

READY IN 10 MINUTES

100g Alaskan salmon fillet
40g kale
30g closed cup mushrooms
5g organic butter
2 medium sized eggs
salt and pepper to season

SERVES 1

In a large shallow pan, bring some water to the boil - just a couple of inches of water is adequate for shallow poaching.

Add the salmon and poach gently for 8 minutes, turning on each side as it cooks.

In a separate saucepan, melt the butter over a medium heat and cook the mushrooms for 3-4 minutes until soft.

Bring a small pan of water to the boil (again just a couple of inches of water). Reduce the heat to a very gentle simmer and carefully add the eggs.

Poach for 2-4 minutes (2 minutes is ideal for a runny egg).

Add the kale to the saucepan with the salmon and cook it in the water for several minutes. Top up with water if necessary.

When the salmon is cooked - it should be a light pink colour throughout - remove it from the saucepan and set aside. Drain the kale and leave for a few minutes to remove excess water.

Place the kale and the mushrooms on a plate and top with the salmon and the eggs. Season well with salt and pepper.

PER SERVING:
457 Calories
6g Carbs
42g Protein
30g Fat

Ryan-Lindsey-Fitness | 07547 192913

BREAKFAST

B.C.T.A.
(Bacon, Chicken, Tomato, Avocado)

RyanLindseyFitness
Be so good they can't ignore you

10g organic butter/organic coconut oil
2 rashers unsmoked bacon (use a vegetarian bacon* if preferred)
2 spring onions, chopped
2 chicken breasts, halved/Quorn meat free chicken*
2 beef tomatoes, cut into slices
half an avocado, mashed

SERVES 2

*Note: Some meat free alternatives contain gluten and/or MSG. Please check the label before you buy!

Suggestion:

Try to use unprocessed bacon, preferably cured with natural ingredients, that contains no added artificial ingredients or preservatives. Try your local butcher or farm shop

In a frying pan, melt the butter or oil over a medium heat. Fry the bacon rashers on both sides until crispy. Remove from pan and put to one side.

Pan fry the chicken for around 6-8 minutes until cooked through. Add the spring onions and fry for one minute. Remove pan from heat.

Arrange the items on a plate in a stack, starting with a piece of chicken as a base, and finishing with another piece of chicken as a 'lid'.

PER SERVING:
476 Calories
9g Carbs
47g Protein
28g Fat

32 LUNCH

Lentil, sweet potato & coriander stew

2 tbsps organic coconut oil
1 small red onion, finely chopped
1 large carrot, finely chopped
1 garlic clove, finely chopped
1 tsp ground coriander
1 tsp celery salt
½ tsp ground cumin
350g red lentils, soaked overnight
1 bay leaf
1 litre cold fresh water
2 medium sized sweet potatoes, peeled and diced
1 x 400g can chopped tomatoes
juice of half a lemon
handful coriander, finely chopped
½ tsp salt
½ tsp black pepper
4 tbsps plain yoghurt for serving
(use dairy free yoghurt if preferred)

SERVES 4

In a large saucepan, heat the oil over a medium heat. Add the onion and carrots. Cook, stirring occasionally, until softened. Add the garlic, ground coriander, celery salt and cumin and cook for 30 seconds. Add the lentils, water and the bay leaf.

Bring to a boil, then reduce to a simmer. Cover and cook for 10 minutes. Add the potatoes and cook for a further 10-15 minutes or until the potatoes are just tender.

Stir in the tomatoes and cook for several minutes until warmed through. Remove the bay leaf. Stir in the lemon juice, coriander, salt and pepper. Spoon into a bowl and top with a spoonful of yoghurt.

PER SERVING:
348 Calories
47g Carbs
13g Protein
12g Fat

Ryan-Lindsey-Fitness | 07547 192913

LUNCH

O-mega salad

1 medium sized egg
3 small new potatoes, chopped into small pieces
1 tsp organic butter
125g fresh chicken breast/Quorn meat free chicken*, cut into strips
½ tsp dried oregano
few handfuls of mixed lettuce, torn into small pieces
¼ red pepper, diced
¼ yellow pepper, diced
4 cherry tomatoes, chopped
small handful samphire
25g cucumber, sliced
1½ tsps organic olive oil
2 tsps omega sprinkle (flaxseed, linseed, sesame seeds, sunflower seeds)
salt and pepper to season

SERVES 1

Bring a saucepan of water to the boil and cook the egg for around 10 minutes. Remove from water and set aside.

Add the potatoes to the water and simmer for 10 minutes or until soft. Remove from the water and drain.

Melt the butter over a medium heat in a frying pan and add the chicken. Sprinkle over the oregano, and cook for around 8 minutes, turning occasionally to brown on all sides. Once cooked, remove chicken from pan and set aside.

In a salad bowl, mix together the lettuce, peppers, tomatoes, samphire and cucumber. Pour over the olive oil and mix well.

Slice the egg into quarters and arrange over the salad leaves, along with the chicken. Top with the omega sprinkle and season with salt and pepper.

Store in an airtight container and refrigerate for up to 24 hours.

***Note:** Some meat free alternatives contain gluten and/or MSG. Please check the label before you buy!*

PER SERVING:
482 Calories
19g Carbs
52g Protein
22g Fat

RyanLindseyFitness
Be so good they can't ignore you

34 LUNCH

Egg drop soup

500ml homemade stock (see recipes on right)
200g fresh chicken breast/Quorn meat free chicken*, diced
300g frozen vegetables, (broccoli, carrots, sweetcorn, beans, etc)
2 medium sized eggs, beaten
3 spring onions, finely sliced
salt and pepper

SERVES 2

READY IN 10 MINUTES

In a large saucepan, bring the stock to a gentle simmer. Add the chicken and vegetables. Simmer rapidly for 5 minutes.

Pour eggs into the soup in a steady stream, then stir gently while the egg cooks. Season with salt and pepper to taste. Spoon into bowls and garnish with spring onions.

PER SERVING:
365 Calories
21g Carbs
41g Protein
13g Fat

* *Note:* Some meat free alternatives contain gluten and/or MSG. Please check the label before you buy!

Home-made chicken stock: Chicken stock is quick to make and so good for you! Place a whole chicken carcass in a large pan full of water (enough to cover the chicken). Season well with salt and pepper and add a bay leaf.

Simmer for 2 hours. Remove from heat and allow to cool completely, then drain the liquid from the carcass. Discard carcass and bay leaf. The stock can be frozen or kept in the fridge for several days

Home-made vegetable stock: Add a drop of olive oil to a large saucepan over a medium heat. Add a large diced white onion, a sliced leek, and chopped carrot and sweat for 2-3 minutes. Add enough cold water to cover the vegetables and turn up the heat to high. Add some finely chopped garlic, one stick of chopped celery, several chopped tomatoes, 1 tsp dried parsley, half a tsp of black pepper, half a tsp salt, 1 tsp dried fennel, a sprig of fresh or 1 tsp dried rosemary.

Stir well, bring to the boil, cover, then reduce to a simmer for 25 minutes. Pour the stock through a sieve. Discard the vegetable pieces or re-use. The liquid stock can be stored in the fridge for up to three days or frozen in batches for future use.

Ryan-Lindsey-Fitness | 07547 192913   LUNCH

Coconut stew

2 small shallots, roughly chopped
75g fresh coconut, grated
2 garlic cloves, finely chopped
3 jalapeno peppers, seeded and halved
1 tbsp organic coconut oil
300g fresh chicken breast/Quorn meat free chicken*, diced
1 large cucumber, peeled, seeded and sliced
1 small cauliflower head, cut into florets
1 large carrot, peeled and sliced
2 spring onions, finely chopped
60g green beans, ends removed
1 tsp turmeric
½ tsp ground cumin
300ml light coconut milk
salt to taste
150g plain yoghurt (use dairy free yoghurt if preferred)

SERVES 3

In a food processor, blend the shallots, fresh coconut, garlic and jalapenos for one minute until finely shredded.

In a large saucepan, warm the coconut oil and add the shredded mixture to the pan. Sauté for two minutes.

Add the chicken and the cucumber, cauliflower, carrot, spring onions, green beans, turmeric and cumin. Sauté for one minute then add coconut milk and bring to a rapid simmer.

Reduce heat slightly, cover and cook for around 8 minutes until vegetables are cooked.

Add salt to taste. Remove from heat and stir in the yoghurt.

***Note:** Some meat free alternatives contain gluten and/or MSG. Please check the label before you buy!

PER SERVING:
425 Calories
21g Carbs
29g Protein
25g Fat

Dill & caper salmon burgers

350g Alaskan salmon fillets
1 tsp dijon mustard
1 tbsp dill, finely chopped
1 tsp capers, drained
1 jalapeno pepper, seeds removed, finely chopped
half a small red onion, finely chopped
¼ tsp rock salt
lemon wedge to garnish
1 tsp organic coconut oil

SERVES 2

Suggestion:

These taste great with a Refreshing Cucumber Salad. See recipe on page 6

Cut the salmon into chunks and put quarter into a food processor with the mustard. Pulse into a smooth paste. Add remaining salmon and ingredients and pulse to break up salmon into small chunks, rather than a smooth paste.

Shape the salmon into two burgers. If the burgers are very moist, brush lightly with coconut flour.

Heat a skillet over a medium heat. Add the coconut oil and fry the burgers gently for 3-5 minutes until firm and easy to flip. Turn and repeat.

Serve with wedges of lemon.

PER SERVING:
464 Calories
3g Carbs
50g Protein
28g Fat

Ryan-Lindsey-Fitness | 07547 192913

LUNCH

Cauliflower chicken

1 large cauliflower head, grated
1 tbsp organic butter/coconut oil
600g boneless chicken thighs/Quorn meat free chicken*, cut into strips
1 medium sized white onion, finely chopped
1 jalapeno pepper, finely chopped
2 garlic cloves, finely chopped
1 green pepper, diced
1 red pepper, diced
1 tin (400g) tomatoes
150ml chicken/vegetable stock (see recipes on page 35)
1 tsp ground cumin
1 tsp salt
100g frozen peas

SERVES 4

Grate the cauliflower or whizz in a food processor.

In a large saucepan, heat the butter or oil over a medium / high heat and add the chicken. Cook for 4-6 minutes until browned all over.

Add more butter or oil if needed, then add the onion, garlic, jalapeno and peppers and cook for several minutes.

Add tomatoes, stock, cumin, salt and cauliflower. Stir well. Simmer covered for 10 minutes, then add peas and simmer for two minutes.

*** Note:** *Some meat free alternatives contain gluten and/or MSG. Please check the label before you buy!*

PER SERVING:
306 Calories
20g Carbs
34g Protein
10g Fat

38 LUNCH

Zingy turkey kebabs

100g low fat Greek yoghurt (use dairy free yoghurt if preferred)
2 tsps fresh lime juice
1 tsp fresh ginger, peeled and finely chopped
1 garlic clove, finely chopped
½ tsp ground cumin
½ tsp turmeric
½ tsp ground black pepper
½ tsp rock salt
3g organic coconut oil, for greasing
500g fresh turkey breasts/Quorn meat free chicken*, cut into 1½ inch thick pieces
pre-soaked wooden skewers

SERVES 3

*Note: Some meat free alternatives contain gluten and/or MSG. Please check the label before you buy!

In a bowl, combine the yoghurt, lime juice, ginger, garlic, cumin, turmeric, pepper and salt. Add the turkey and marinate in fridge for 30 minutes.

Grease an oven tray with a small layer of melted coconut oil and prepare a medium grill.

Thread the turkey onto the skewers. Grill on a medium setting, turning occasionally for 10-12 minutes.

Suggestion:

These taste great with a Refreshing Cucumber Salad. See recipe on page 6

PER SERVING:
317 Calories
5g Carbs
54g Protein
9g Fat

Ryan-Lindsey-Fitness | 07547 192913

LUNCH 39

Sesame chicken

2 tbsps organic coconut oil
350g chicken breast/Quorn meat free chicken*, cut into strips
salt and pepper
1 tbsp olive oil
1 tbsp tahini
1 tbsp sherry vinegar
2 small carrots, grated
12 radishes, sliced
handful parsley, roughly chopped
1 tsp sesame seeds to garnish

SERVES 2

Note: Some meat free alternatives contain gluten and/or MSG. Please check the label before you buy!

Melt half of the coconut oil gently in a pan.

Season the chicken with salt and pepper and mix with the melted oil. In a skillet, melt the remaining oil over a medium/high heat.

Cook the chicken for 10 minutes. Set aside to cool slightly.

In a jug, combine the tahini, oil and sherry vinegar.

In a bowl, mix the chicken with carrots, radish and parsley. Drizzle the tahini dressing on top and mix well.

Garnish with sesame seeds.

PER SERVING:
446 Calories
11g Carbs
42g Protein
26g Fat

40 LUNCH

Chicken meatballs

350g fresh chicken breast/Quorn meat free chicken*, diced
1 large carrot, grated
2 garlic cloves
100g fresh coconut, grated
1 egg
2 tsp curry powder
½ tsp salt
handful parsley or coriander
10g organic coconut oil

MAKES 20 MEATBALLS

Put everything except for the coconut oil into a food processor and whizz into a smooth paste. Using your hands, form 20 meatballs.

In a large pan, melt the coconut oil over a high heat. When the oil is hot, put the meatballs in the pan and cook for 2 minutes. Roll each meatball over and cook for a further 5 minutes.

Reduce to a medium heat, cover the pan and cook for a further 6-8 minutes.

***Note:** Some meat free alternatives contain gluten and/or MSG. Please check the label before you buy!

Suggestion:
These are ideal as a portable snack, or as a meal served with a healthy accompaniment, such as a salad and sweet potato

PER MEATBALL:
51 Calories
1g Carbs
5g Protein
3g Fat

Ryan-Lindsey-Fitness | 07547 192913

LUNCH

Fiery fries

350g all rounder potatoes peeled and cut into chips
1½ tbsps olive oil
2 tsps paprika
good pinch of sea salt
2 tsps chilli flakes

SERVES 2

Preheat oven to 170°C.

Bring a large pan of lightly salted water to the boil.

Add the potatoes and cook for around 8 minutes, so that they are still quite firm.

Remove pan from heat and drain carefully.

Place a sheet of foil on a baking tray.

Drizzle with half of the oil and sprinkle with the paprika, salt and chilli flakes.

Add the potatoes and turn over so they get a coating of spices and oil. Drizzle over the remaining oil.

Cook for 20 minutes, then turn the chips over.

Cook for a further 20-25 minutes until golden and crispy.

PER SERVING:
222 Calories
29g Carbs
4g Protein
10g Fat

Salmon asparagus

4-6 asparagus spears
1 tbsp organic butter/ organic coconut oil
2 x 150g Alaskan salmon steaks
½ tsp Himalayan or rock salt
pepper to season
15 cherry tomatoes
2 lemon wedges

SERVES 2

Bring a small pan of salted water to the boil. Add the asparagus, reduce heat and simmer for around 3 minutes. Drain the asparagus and cool in cold water.

In a heavy skillet, melt the butter or oil over a medium heat. Add the salmon and cook for 10 minutes (turning halfway).

Season with the salt and pepper. Add the cherry tomatoes to the pan, and cook for 1-2 minutes. Check that the salmon is cooked through (the meat should now be a lighter colour all the way through).

Remove pan from heat. Serve the salmon with the asparagus and tomatoes.

Garnish with a wedge of lemon.

PER SERVING:
369 Calories
6g Carbs
30g Protein
25g Fat

Steak strip salad

READY IN 10 MINUTES

½ tbsp organic coconut oil
100g stir fry steak, cut into strips
handful fresh spinach
handful cherry tomatoes
5 radishes, cut into small pieces
75g cucumber, chopped roughly
salt and pepper
1 tbsp extra virgin olive oil
1 tsp organic balsamic vinegar

SERVES 1

Heat the coconut oil in a frying pan to a medium/high heat and add the steak.

Season well and cook for 3-5 minutes on both sides, until cooked. Remove pan from heat.

In a bowl, add the spinach, tomatoes, radishes and cucumber. Top with the steak.

Pour the oil into a jug. Add the balsamic vinegar, then spoon the dressing onto the salad.

PER SERVING:
365 Calories
9g Carbs
35g Protein
21g Fat

Tuna & sweet potato crunchy salad

READY IN 10 MINUTES

10g organic butter/coconut oil
1 small white onion, diced
130g tinned tuna chunks, drained
1 medium sized sweet potato
handful mixed leaf lettuce
75g cucumber, chopped roughly
1 red pepper, sliced
1 beef tomato, diced
2 tbsps extra virgin olive oil
1 tsp balsamic vinegar
juice of half a lemon

SERVES 1

PER SERVING:
539 Calories
49g Carbs
43g Protein
19g Fat

Melt the butter or oil gently a frying pan and add the onion. Cook over a medium heat until softened. Remove from heat and place in a bowl. Add the tuna and mix well.

Pierce the potato with a knife and microwave on full heat for 6-8 minutes. When cooked, mash in a bowl with a fork. Place the potato in a serving bowl. Add the lettuce, cucumber, red pepper and tomato.

Pour the oil into a jug. Add the balsamic vinegar, then spoon the dressing onto the salad. Top with tuna and drizzle with lemon juice.

Ryan-Lindsey-Fitness | 07547 192913

LUNCH

Lentil pepper soup

250g red lentils
2 pints cold water or vegetable/chicken stock (see recipes on page 35)
half a large white onion, chopped
3 garlic cloves, chopped
1½ tsp cumin
½ tsp ground coriander
½ tsp paprika
1 bay leaf
3 medium carrots, peeled and diced
1 red pepper, diced
1 large red onion, finely sliced
juice of half a lemon
¼ teaspoon black pepper

SERVES 4

In a large saucepan set over high heat, bring lentils and stock/water to a boil.

Stir in white onion, garlic, spices and bay leaf. Reduce heat to medium/low.

Cover and simmer. Stir the carrots and red pepper into the soup.

Continue to simmer, covered, for around 15 minutes until the carrots are tender.

Stir in red onion, lemon juice and black pepper.

Cook for a further 10 minutes. Serve immediately.

PER SERVING:
224 Calories
34g Carbs
13g Protein
4g Fat

Egg & ham salad

10 green beans, ends removed
2 medium sized eggs
handful lettuce leaves
2 slices ham (use a vegetarian ham* alternative if preferred)
8 cherry tomatoes
75g cucumber, sliced
3 spring onions, chopped
1 tsp extra virgin olive oil
1 tsp balsamic vinegar
sprinkle salad seasoning**

SERVES 1

***Note:** Some meat free alternatives contain gluten and/or MSG. Please check the label before you buy!

** See recipe on page 28

PER SERVING:
353 Calories
12g Carbs
29g Protein
21g Fat

Bring a small pan of salted water to the boil. Add the green beans and simmer gently for 3 minutes. Remove from the water with a serrated spoon.

Return the pan of water to the boil. Add the eggs and simmer gently for 10 minutes. Remove from heat and cool with cold water for several minutes. Peel eggs and slice.

In a bowl add the lettuce, ham, eggs, tomatoes, cucumber, beans and spring onions.

Pour the oil into a jug. Add the balsamic vinegar, then spoon the dressing onto the salad.

Sprinkle with salad seasoning.

Ryan-Lindsey-Fitness | 07547 192913

Hambled eggs

2 medium sized eggs
30g ham, cut into small pieces
(use a vegetarian ham* alternative if preferred)
handful cherry tomatoes
salt and pepper

SERVES 1

***Note:** Some meat free alternatives contain gluten and/or MSG. Please check the label before you buy!

Suggestion:
Try to use unprocessed ham, which is free from artificial ingredients and preservatives

READY IN 10 MINUTES

RyanLindseyFitness
Be so good they can't ignore you

Crack the eggs into a frying pan over a medium heat. Add the ham and tomatoes and stir continuously with a wooden spoon. Season well.

When the eggs are cooked, remove from heat and serve.

PER SERVING:
246 Calories
4g Carbs
26g Protein
14g Fat

48 LUNCH

Mackerel salad

READY IN 10 MINUTES

handful lettuce leaves
5 cherry tomatoes
5 radishes, chopped
½ pepper, any colour, sliced
75g cucumber, sliced
3 spring onions, chopped
100g peppered mackerel
1 tsp extra virgin olive oil
1 tsp balsamic vinegar
sprinkle salad seasoning*

SERVES 1

*See recipe on page 28

In a bowl add the lettuce, tomatoes, radishes, pepper, cucumber and spring onions.

Using your hands, gently tear the mackerel into large chunks. Add to the salad.

Pour the oil into a jug. Add the balsamic vinegar, and spoon the dressing onto the salad.

Sprinkle with salad seasoning.

PER SERVING:
480 Calories
15g Carbs
24g Protein
36g Fat

Ryan-Lindsey-Fitness | 07547 192913

LUNCH

Tomato & basil soup

1 tsp organic butter/coconut oil
1½ large white onions, finely chopped
2 garlic cloves, finely chopped
2 small sticks celery, chopped
2 small potatoes, peeled and diced
2 medium sized carrots, peeled and chopped
2 medium sized tomatoes, diced
1 pint vegetable stock (see recipe on page 35)
1 x 400g can chopped tomatoes
1 sprig fresh basil, roughly chopped
salt and pepper

SERVES 4

In a large pan, gently melt the butter or oil and cook the onion until softened.

Add the garlic, celery, potato and carrots and cook for 3-4 minutes. Add the diced tomatoes and cook for a further two minutes.

Add the stock and tinned tomatoes. Simmer over a gentle heat for 45 minutes. Remove from heat and allow to cool.

Add the basil, and season well with salt and pepper, then whizz everything in a food processor for just long enough to get the big lumps out.

The soup can be reheated to serve, kept in the fridge for up to 4 days or frozen on the same day.

PER SERVING:
200 Calories
33g Carbs
8g Protein
4g Fat

Protein rich omelette

3 medium sized eggs
½ tsp organic butter/coconut oil
1 rasher bacon, cut into small pieces (use a vegetarian bacon* alternative if preferred)
5 closed cup mushrooms, peeled and sliced
75g cooked chicken breast/Quorn meat free chicken*, diced
1 beef tomato, sliced
handful spinach

SERVES 1

Suggestion:

Try to use unprocessed bacon, preferably cured with natural ingredients, that contains no added artificial ingredients or preservatives. Try your local butcher or farm shop

Note: Some meat free alternatives contain gluten and/or MSG. Please check the label before you buy!

Add the chicken pieces to the pan and cook for several minutes until heated through. Remove from heat and set aside.

Add the tomato to the pan and cook gently for 1-2 minutes on each side until softened.

Remove any bits from the pan and melt the remaining butter or oil over a medium/high heat, ensuring there is an even glaze over the base of the pan. Add the eggs and allow to cook for 3-4 minutes until the edges of the mixture start to crisp. When the centre of the omelette starts to cook, add the bacon, mushrooms, tomatoes, chicken over one half of the egg mixture. Add the spinach. Cook for several minutes.

Using a wooden spoon with a flat edge, turn the empty side of the omelette up and fold over the spinach. Remove the omelette from heat and serve.

Break the eggs into a jug and beat with a fork. Melt half of the butter or oil in a frying pan and cook the bacon over a medium/high heat until crispy. Remove bacon from heat and set aside.

Reduce pan to medium heat. Add the mushrooms and cook for 5 minutes. Remove from heat and set aside.

PER SERVING:
505 Calories
9g Carbs
52g Protein
29g Fat

Ryan-Lindsey-Fitness | 07547 192913

5 veg omelette

3 medium sized eggs plus
1 egg white, beaten
10g organic butter
2 medium sized mushrooms, sliced
3 medium sized broccoli florets, finely chopped
30g red pepper, finely chopped
2 spring onions, finely chopped
Himalayan sea salt to season
handful baby leaf spinach, roughly chopped
10g low fat cheddar cheese, grated (use dairy free cheese if preferred)

SERVES 2

Break the eggs and whites into a jug and beat with a fork and season well.

Melt half of the butter in a non-stick frying pan over a medium heat and add all of the chopped vegetables except for the spinach.

Sauté for 5 minutes, until softened. Remove from heat and set aside.

Remove any bits from the pan. Melt the remaining butter. Pour the eggs into the pan. Cook gently for around 3-4 minutes until the edges of the mixture start to crisp.

When the centre of the omelette begins to firm up, add the spinach over the entire omelette. Then carefully add the other vegetables on top of the spinach, so that it wilts. Cook for around 1-2 minutes.

Add the cheese. Using a wooden slice fold the omelette in half. Remove the omelette from the pan and serve.

Any leftovers can be kept in the fridge for up to 3 days.

PER SERVING:
210 Calories
4g Carbs
17g Protein
14g Fat

Quick, easy, tasty soup

10g organic butter
1 medium sized white onion, finely chopped
3 medium sized carrots, sliced
2 large sticks celery, finely chopped
800g chicken breast/Quorn meat free chicken*, diced
2 garlic cloves, crushed
1 tsp paprika
1 tsp ground cumin
½ tsp Himalayan pink salt
1 tsp dried thyme
1 x 400g can chopped tomatoes
1 medium salad tomato, diced
15g tomato purée
1 pint chicken or vegetable stock (see recipes on page 35)
1 red pepper, sliced
200g mixed beans, drained

SERVES 4

* **Note:** *Some meat free alternatives contain gluten and/or MSG. Please check the label before you buy!*

Add the chicken, garlic, spices, salt and thyme. Cook stirring for 10 minutes.

Add the tomatoes, purée, stock and red pepper. Bring to a simmer and cook uncovered for 50 minutes.

Add the mixed beans and cook for a further 5 minutes.

Once cooled, this can be kept in the fridge for up to 4 days or frozen on the same day.

Heat the butter in a large pan. Add the onion and cook gently until softened. Add the carrot and celery and cook for 5 minutes, stirring regularly.

PER SERVING:
290 Calories
16g Carbs
43g Protein
6g Fat

Ryan-Lindsey-Fitness | 07547 192913

LUNCH

Buzzing curry

1 tbsp cumin seeds
2 tbsps ghee
5 medium sized white onions, finely diced
1 clove garlic, finely chopped
2 tbsps fresh ginger, peeled and finely chopped
handful green finger chillis, finely chopped
600g extra lean beef, diced/ low fat Quorn mince*
2 tbsps ground turmeric
1 tbsp garam masala
1 tbsp meat masala
1 tbsp rock salt
handful curry leaves (optional)
1 x 400g can chopped tomatoes
50ml cold fresh water
fresh coriander, chopped
30g per person uncooked basmati rice
30g per person cauliflower, finely chopped or grated

SERVES 4

*** Note:** *Some meat free alternatives contain gluten and/or MSG. Please check the label before you buy!*

In a large pan, heat the cumin seeds gently for 30-45 seconds, until you can smell them roasting. Add the ghee and heat until melted, then add the onions. Cook on a medium heat until softened.

Stir in the garlic, ginger and chillis. Cook for one minute. Add the beef/Quorn and cook for two minutes. Add the spices, rock salt and curry leaves. Stir well, then add the tomatoes, and water and simmer for 1 hour. Add more water if necessary. Cook for 1 hour over a medium heat.

Meanwhile place the rice in a large saucepan of cold salted water and bring to the boil. Simmer the rice gently until almost cooked then add the cauliflower and cook for 2 minutes.

Drain and serve garnished with coriander.

PER SERVING:
500 Calories
48g Carbs
41g Protein
16g Fat

54 DINNER

Mediterranean salmon

10g organic butter/coconut oil
2 cloves garlic, finely chopped
1 small red onion, finely chopped
1 x 400g can chopped tomatoes
½ pint chicken or vegetable stock
(see recipes on page 35)
125g bulgur wheat
salt and pepper
2 x 150g Alaskan salmon fillets
handful fresh coriander,
finely chopped
wedge lemon to garnish

SERVES 2

Preheat oven to 150°C.

In a large pan, melt one third of the butter or oil over a medium heat and cook the garlic and onion until softened. Add the tomatoes and cook for 5 minutes. Add the stock and continue to cook.

Meanwhile, melt half of the remaining butter or oil in a frying pan over a medium heat. Gently fry the bulgur wheat for one minute. Pour the bulgur wheat into an overproof dish.

Add the mixture from the large pan and stir well. Season well with salt and pepper. Cook in the oven for 15 minutes.

Meanwhile, heat a skillet over a medium temperature. Melt the remaining butter or oil and fry the salmon for 8-10 minutes turning half way. When the flesh is a pale pink all the way through, remove from the heat.

Remove the bulgur wheat mixture from the oven. Stir in the coriander.

To serve, spoon half of the bulgur wheat mixture onto a plate. Add the cooked salmon and garnish with a wedge of lemon.

PER SERVING:
624 Calories
59g Carbs
43g Protein
24g Fat

Ryan-Lindsey-Fitness | 07547 192913

Chicken, rice & pepper pot

1 tbsp organic coconut oil
1 whole chicken, jointed, or 8 chicken pieces
1 large white onion, chopped
1 large stick celery, finely chopped
1 red pepper, diced
3 garlic cloves, crushed
1 tbsp tomato purée
1 tbsp dried thyme
1½ pts chicken stock (see recipe on page 35)
150g long grain rice (dry weight)
150g cauliflower, finely chopped
salt and pepper

SERVES 4

Melt the oil over a medium/high heat in a large saucepan. Brown the chicken pieces on all sides. You may have to do this in batches. Remove from the dish and put to one side.

Lower the heat, add the onion, celery and pepper and gently cook for 10 minutes until softened. Add the garlic and cook for a further 2 minutes. Stir in the tomato purée and cook for 1 minute.

Return the chicken pieces to the dish along with the thyme and stock. Bring the liquid to a boil, cover the dish with a tight-fitting lid and lower the heat. Cook for 30 minutes.

Tip in the rice and stir well. Cover, set over a low heat and cook for a further 15 minutes, or until the rice is cooked and has absorbed most of the liquid.

Add the cauliflower and cook for a further 5 minutes. Remove from the heat and leave the dish to sit for 10 minutes to absorb any of the remaining liquid. Season to taste.

PER SERVING:
418 Calories
48g Carbs
27g Protein
6g Fat

Warming stew

1 tbsp ghee
1 small white onion, finely chopped
850g lean casserole beef/tofu*
handful button mushrooms, sliced
3 cloves garlic, finely chopped
2 medium sized carrots, peeled and chopped
half a swede, diced
375g small all purpose potatoes, peeled and chopped
1 organic stock cube dissolved in 1 pint boiling water
sprig fresh rosemary
1 tbsp tomato purée
salt and pepper to season

SERVES 4

*Note: Some meat free alternatives contain gluten and/or MSG. Please check the label before you buy!

In a large saucepan, melt the ghee over a medium heat. Add the onion, and sauté gently until soft. Transfer to a separate plate.

Add the beef, if using, to the saucepan and brown on all sides (approximately 3-5 minutes). If using tofu, cook gently for around 4-5 minutes until soft. Transfer to a separate plate.

Add the mushrooms to the saucepan and cook for 3-5 minutes until soft. Add the garlic and cook for a further 2 minutes, stirring continuously.

Return the beef/tofu and onions back into the saucepan. Stir in the carrots, swede and potatoes and add the stock liquid. There should be enough liquid in the pan to cook the vegetables, although they needn't be completely covered.

Add the rosemary and tomato purée and season well. Cover and simmer for up to two hours (if using beef) or 45 minutes if using tofu. Top up with fresh water if necessary. As the potatoes cook, they will thicken up the sauce.

PER SERVING: with beef/with tofu
501 Calories/393 Calories
29g Carbs/32g Carbs
76g Protein/19g Protein
9g Fat/21g Fat

Ryan-Lindsey-Fitness | 07547 192913

DINNER

Authentic curry

1 tbsp cumin seeds
1 tbsp ghee/coconut oil
5 medium sized onions, diced
5-10 garlic cloves, finely chopped
1-2 inch piece fresh ginger, peeled and finely chopped
5 green chillis, finely chopped
600g fresh chicken breast/Quorn meat free chicken*, diced
2 tbsps ground turmeric
1 tbsp garam masala
1 tbsp meat masala
1 tbsp rock salt
1 tin (400g) plum tomatoes
50ml cold fresh water
60g per person uncooked basmati rice
30g per person cauliflower, finely chopped or grated
handful fresh coriander

SERVES 4

Note: Some meat free alternatives contain gluten and/or MSG. Please check the label before you buy!

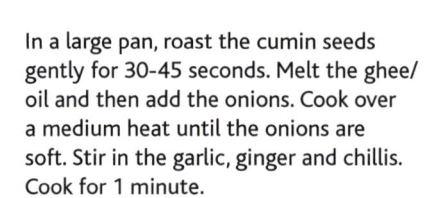

PER SERVING:
416 Calories
47g Carbs
39g Protein
8g Fat

In a large pan, roast the cumin seeds gently for 30-45 seconds. Melt the ghee/oil and then add the onions. Cook over a medium heat until the onions are soft. Stir in the garlic, ginger and chillis. Cook for 1 minute.

Add the chicken and cook for 2 minutes. Then add the spices and rock salt. Stir well, coating the meat in the spices. Add the tin of tomatoes, and the water and simmer for 10 minutes. Add more water if the mixture seems too dry. Cover and simmer for one hour.

Meanwhile, add the rice to a pan of cold salted water and bring to the boiil. Simmer gently until almost cooked, then add the cauliflower and cook for 2 minutes.

Drain and serve garnished with coriander.

Spaghetti courgetti

1 tbsp olive oil
3 large white onions, finely chopped
fresh basil leaves and stalks, chopped roughly
500g lean beef mince/low fat Quorn mince*
100g mushrooms, sliced
1 salad tomato, diced
1 stick celery, finely chopped
½ green pepper, diced
4 cloves garlic, finely chopped
dollop of tomato purée
4 large courgettes
1 x 400g can chopped tomatoes
salt and pepper to season
sprig fresh basil to garnish

SERVES 4

Note: Some meat free alternatives contain gluten and/or MSG. Please check the label before you buy!

In a frying pan, gently heat the oil over a low/medium heat. Fry the onions until soft. Add the chopped basil and fry for 30 seconds. Add the mince and season well with salt and pepper. When the mince is browned, add the mushrooms, salad tomato, celery, pepper and garlic.

Cook gently for 5 minutes. Add the tin of tomatoes and tomato purée. Cook over a medium heat for 20 minutes.

Chop the courgettes into fine spaghetti strips, or wider tagliatelle size strips. Bring to the boil in a pan of salted water, and simmer gently for several minutes. Serve the sauce on a bed of courgette spaghetti. Garnish with a sprig of basil.

PER SERVING:
388 Calories
20g Carbs
32g Protein
20g Fat

Ryan-Lindsey-Fitness | 07547 192913

DINNER

Lentil & sweet potato curry

2 tbsps olive oil
2 medium sized white onions, finely chopped
pinch of rock salt
2 sweet potatoes, peeled and cut into 1 inch chunks
1 inch piece fresh ginger, peeled and finely chopped
2 small garlic cloves, chopped
1 tbsp curry powder
1 bay leaf
150g red lentils (dry weight)
500ml boiling water

SERVES 3

Warm the oil in a large saucepan over a gentle heat. Add the onion and a pinch of salt and sauté, stirring occasionally, until the onion softens.

Add the sweet potato, ginger, garlic, curry powder and bay leaf and sauté for one minute until fragrant.

Add the boiling water and stir in the lentils. Reduce the heat to medium-low, cover and simmer for around 18-20 minutes, until the lentils break down and the sweet potatoes are tender.

Season with salt and serve.

PER SERVING:
348 Calories
47g Carbs
13g Protein
12g Fat

Chickpea stew

1 tbsp olive oil
600g chicken fillets/Quorn meat free chicken*, diced
2 orange peppers, diced
1 large white onion, finely chopped
3 cloves garlic, finely chopped
1 tsp ground cumin
1 tsp ground coriander
2 red chillis, deseeded
1 x 400g can chickpeas, drained and rinsed
500ml chicken or vegetable stock (see recipes on page 35)
30g per person uncooked basmati rice
30g per person cauliflower, finely chopped or grateed
handful fresh coriander

SERVES 4

Preheat oven to 190°C.

Heat the oil to a medium/low heat in a large saucepan. Fry the chicken until golden. Remove chicken from pan and set aside.

Add the peppers, onion, garlic, spices and chillis and fry gently for 5 minutes.

Return the chicken to the saucepan and add the chickpeas and stock. Transfer the contents of the saucepan to a casserole dish, cover and cook in the oven for 20 minutes. Add the rice and cook for a further 10-15 minutes (if using white rice) or 15-20 minutes (brown rice).

Add the cauliflower and cook for a further 5 minutes. Drain and serve.

***Note:** Some meat free alternatives contain gluten and/or MSG. Please check the label before you buy!

PER SERVING:
350 Calories
45g Carbs
47g Protein
13g Fat

Ryan-Lindsey-Fitness | 07547 192913

DINNER

Chicken nuggets

1 tsp coconut flour
15g ground almonds
pinch of paprika
salt and pepper to season
1 tsp organic coconut oil
1 medium sized egg
200g fresh chicken breast/Quorn meat free chicken*, diced

MAKES 10 NUGGETS

***Note:** Some meat free alternatives contain gluten and/or MSG. Please check the label before you buy!

Preheat the oven to 180°C.

Mix the flour, almonds, paprika, salt and pepper in a bowl.

In a separate bowl whisk the egg.

Take a piece of chicken and dip it in the egg, coating it evenly. Then dip it in the flour mixture and roll until covered.

Repeat this step with all of the chicken.

Melt the oil in a non stick frying pan over a medium/high heat. Add the chicken and cook for 5 minutes, turning regularly until brown all over.

Transfer the chicken to an oven tray and cook in the oven for 10-15 minutes until cooked through.

PER NUGGET:
46 Calories
0g Carbs
6g Protein
2g Fat

62 DINNER

Chilli con cauli

1 tbsp olive oil
2 large white onions, finely chopped
500g lean beef mince/low fat Quorn mince*
½ green pepper, diced
3 beef tomatoes, diced
5 garlic cloves, finely chopped
4 red or green chilli peppers
1 x 400g can chopped tomatoes
15g tomato purée
1 tsp cayenne pepper
1 x 400g can kidney beans, drained
50g per person uncooked basmati rice
1 medium sized cauliflower head, finely chopped
salt and pepper

SERVES 4

* Note: Some meat free alternatives contain gluten and/or MSG. Please check the label before you buy!

Heat the oil in a pan to a medium heat and add the onion. Fry for several minutes until soft. Add the mince and brown all over. Season well with salt and pepper.

Add the green pepper and beef tomatoes, and cook for several minutes until soft.

PER SERVING:
362 Calories
33g Carbs
35g Protein
10g Fat

Add the garlic cloves and chilli peppers and cook for one minute.

Add the tinned tomatoes, tomato purée and cayenne pepper.

Simmer gently for 15-20 minutes. Add the kidney beans and continue to cook for 10 minutes.

For the Cauli Rice:

Add the rice to a pan of cold salted water and bring to the boil. Simmer gently until cooked, then add the cauliflower. Cook for two minutes before draining.

Serve the chilli sauce on a bed of cauliflower rice.

Ryan-Lindsey-Fitness | 07547 192913   DINNER

Fragrant fish stir fry

100ml light unsweeteened coconut milk
1 tbsp fish sauce (nam pla)
juice of one lime
2 tbsps soy sauce
1 tsp chilli flakes
2 tsps acacia honey
30g per person uncooked basmati rice
30g per person cauliflower, finely chopped
1 tbsp organic coconut oil, melted
1 large red onion, finely chopped
5-6 cloves garlic, finely chopped
1-2 inch piece fresh ginger, peeled and sliced
1 red chilli, sliced
1 small carrot, sliced
handful mushrooms, (any variety) sliced
400g white fish, broken into chunks
60g broccoli, sliced
1 red pepper, sliced
handful beansprouts

SERVES 2

To make the sauce, combine the coconut milk, fish sauce, lime juice, soy sauce, chilli flakes and honey in a bowl. Adjust these flavours to suit your taste, adding more lime juice if too sweet or salty.

Place the rice in a large saucepan of cold salted water and bring to the boil. Simmer gently until cooked then add the cauliflower. Cook for two minutes before draining.

Warm a wok or large frying pan over medium/high heat. Add the coconut oil followed by the onion, garlic, ginger, and chilli. Stir fry for 1-2 minutes, then add the carrot and mushrooms. Also add a quarter of the sauce. Continue stir frying for several minutes.

Add the fish, broccoli, red pepper and beansprouts plus up to half of remaining stir fry sauce. Simmer fish and vegetables in the sauce for up to 5 minutes, until the fish is cooked. Add more of the stir fry sauce as needed, enough to just cover the vegetables in sauce. Simmer for 2 minutes. Remove from heat and serve with rice.

PER SERVING:
591 Calories
53g Carbs
52g Protein
19g Fat

Quick fish stew

10g organic butter/coconut oil
2 garlic cloves, finely chopped
1½ tsps ground cumin
1 tsp paprika
1 tsp Himalayan salt
250ml cold fresh water
1 x 400g can chopped tomatoes
8 cherry tomatoes
1 green pepper, deseeded and cut into chunks
1kg white fish fillets, cut into chunks
60g fresh coriander, finely chopped
1 lemon cut into four wedges

SERVES 5

PER SERVING:
253 Calories
6g Carbs
46g Protein
5g Fat

Heat butter or oil in a large saucepan.

Add the garlic and stir well. Cook for 30 seconds.

Add the cumin, paprika and salt and cook for one minute, stirring continuously.

Add the water and tomatoes. Bring to the boil, then reduce to a simmer.

Add the pepper, and simmer for 5 minutes.

Add the fish and cherry tomatoes and cook for 10 minutes until the fish falls apart. Break the fish up with a wooden spoon.

Stir in the coriander and remove from heat. Serve with a wedge of lemon.

Suggestion:

Tastes great with a serving of fresh green leafy vegetables, such as spinach or kale

Thai red curry

1 tbsp organic coconut oil
¼ jar red Thai paste
1 x 400ml can light unsweetened coconut milk
300g chicken breast/meat free chicken*, diced
handful closed cup mushrooms, sliced
1 aubergine, quartered lengthways and cut into strips
handful baby sweetcorn
handful sugar snap peas
handful cherry tomatoes
30g per person uncooked basmati rice
30g per person cauliflower, finely chopped or grated

SERVES 2

***Note:** Some meat free alternatives contain gluten and/or MSG. Please check the label before you buy!

Heat the coconut oil in a large frying pan over a medium heat. Add the red Thai paste and cook for one minute stirring constantly.

Add the coconut milk and bring to the boil. Reduce heat and simmer.

Add the chicken, mushrooms, aubergine, sweetcorn, peas and tomatoes and cook gently for 15 minutes.

Bring a small saucepan of cold salted water to the boil. Add the rice and simmer gently until almost cooked. Add the cauliflower and cook for 2 minutes.

Drain and serve.

PER SERVING:
424 Calories
56g Carbs
29g Protein
28g Fat

Sizzle steak

2 tsps barbecue seasoning mix
1 sweet potato
1 tsp organic butter/coconut oil
150g steak strips
1 medium sized carrot, peeled and sliced
80g broccoli, cut into florets

SERVES 1

Top Tip:

There are plenty of seasoning mixes available in the markets and stores. Just check the ingredients before you buy and try to avoid anything high in sugar.

Alternatively, why not have a go at making your own spice blend? Try some of these as a start: salt, pepper, onion powder, chilli powder, garlic powder and paprika. Any leftovers can be stored in an airtight container

Rub the barbecue seasoning into both sides of the steak.

Pierce the potato with a knife and microwave on full heat for 6-8 minutes. Cut the potato in half and mash the insides gently with a fork.

In a frying pan melt the butter or oil over a medium heat. Add the steak and cook for several minutes on each side.

Bring a small pan of salted water to the boil. Add the carrots and simmer gently for 3 minutes. Add the broccoli and simmer for a further two minutes. Drain the vegetables.

Serve the steak on a plate with the sweet potato and vegetables.

PER SERVING:
396 Calories
35g Carbs
37g Protein
12g Fat

Ryan-Lindsey-Fitness | 07547 192913

DINNER

Cheating stir fry

In a wok, heat the oil over a medium heat. Add the pork/tofu and cook for 4-5 minutes until cooked through.

Add the vegetables and cook for a further 4 minutes.

Finally, add the sauce and stir well. Cook for 1 minute and serve immediately.

* Note: Some meat free alternatives contain gluten and/or MSG. Please check the label before you buy!

Top Tip:

Look for stir fry sauces which have a low sugar content. The further down the ingredients list the sugar appears, the lower the sugar content.

Avoid any sauces which list sugar at the top of the list

1 tbsp olive oil
300g stir fry pork/tofu*, diced
1 sachet Thai stir fry sauce
450g stir fry vegetables (pre-chopped)

SERVES 2

PER SERVING: with pork/with tofu
419 Calories/403 Calories
22g Carbs/23g Carbs
40g Protein/17g Protein
19g Fat/27g fat

RyanLindseyFitness
Be so good they can't ignore you

68 DINNER

Hot Thai pie

1 tbsp organic butter/coconut oil
2 large white onions, finely chopped
500g turkey mince/low fat Quorn mince*
2 garlic cloves, finely chopped
2 shallots, finely chopped
1 stick fresh lemongrass, minced
1 tbsp galangal, minced (optional)
10 cherry tomatoes, chopped
3 green finger chillis
5 lime leaves
1 tsp chilli flakes
1 x 400ml can light unsweetened coconut milk
1 large all-purpose potato, cut into 1 inch thick cubes
1 cauliflower head, grated
salt and white pepper

SERVES 4

PER SERVING:
436 Calories
28g Carbs
36g Protein
20g Fat

** **Note:** Some meat free alternatives contain gluten and/or MSG. Please check the label before you buy!*

In a large pan, melt the butter or oil and fry the onion until softened. Add the turkey/Quorn mince and cook gently until browned. Season well.

Add the garlic, shallots, lemongrass and galangal and cook for 1 minute. Add the tomatoes, chillis, lime leaves, chilli flakes and most of the coconut milk (reserving a few tablespoons for the mash).

Season well and simmer for 10-15 minutes. Preheat the oven to 160°C.

Bring a saucepan of salted water to the boil and cook the potato for 10 minutes. Add the cauliflower and cook for a further 2 minutes. Drain well, return to the saucepan and mash with a fork. You may want to add a small amount of butter or olive oil to soften up the mash. When all the lumps are gone, add the remaining coconut milk to the mash. Season well.

Spoon the mince into a rectangular oven dish. Top with the mash. Cook for 45 minutes and serve.

Ryan-Lindsey-Fitness | 07547 192913

Spinach & ricotta pizza

small amount of organic coconut oil/butter to grease dish
4 medium sized eggs
3 egg whites
40g porridge oats (use gluten free oats if preferred)
4 cherry tomatoes, halved
40g baby leaf spinach, finely chopped
1 red chilli pepper, finely chopped
½ a green pepper, finely chopped
1 tsp paprika
1 tsp dried oregano
40g low fat ricotta/cream cheese (use dairy free cheese if preferred)
salt and pepper to season

MAKES 6 SLICES

Suggestion:

This recipe tastes great either warm from the oven or straight from the fridge. Makes a great portable snack.

Preheat oven to 150°C.

Lightly grease a large round ovenproof dish with coconut oil or butter.

Whisk the eggs and egg whites in a jug. Season well.

Add the oats, vegetables, dried spices and herbs and stir well.

Pour into the dish and cook for around 10 minutes, until centre of mixture is cooked.

Spoon on the ricotta cheese, and cook for a further 5 minutes.

Once cooled, store any leftovers in the fridge for up to 3 days.

PER SLICE:
93 Calories
6g Carbs
9g Protein
4g Fat

DINNER

Mediterranean chicken

1 tbsp organic coconut oil
1kg fresh chicken breast/Quorn meat free chicken*, diced
Himalayan pink salt to taste
1 tbsp paprika
2 tsps cayenne pepper
6 small red onions, finely chopped
4 cloves garlic, finely chopped
2 tbsps tomato purée

SERVES 6

***Note:** Some meat free alternatives contain gluten and/or MSG. Please check the label before you buy!

Heat the oil in a pan over a medium heat.

Add the chicken and cook for five minutes, stirring regularly.

Add the salt, spices and stir.

Add the onion, garlic and tomato purée.

Stir well and simmer for 15-20 minutes until the chicken is cooked through.

Serve with fresh vegetables and sweet potato or basmati rice.

PER SERVING:
313 Calories
6g Carbs
52g Protein
9g Fat

Ryan-Lindsey-Fitness | 07547 192913

Mince masala

2 tsps organic coconut oil
1 large white onion, finely chopped
750g extra lean beef mince/ low fat Quorn mince*
3 cloves garlic, finely chopped
2 tsps Mangal meat masala spice
1 tsp cayenne pepper
1 tsp pink Himalayan salt
2 tbsps tomato purée

SERVES 4

* *Note:* Some meat free alternatives contain gluten and/or MSG. Please check the label before you buy!

Suggestion:

Meat masala tastes great with a side of chopped raw baby leaf spinach and chopped cherry tomatoes

Melt the oil over a medium heat. Add the onions and cook for five minutes until soft.

Add the mince and stir frequently until browned all over. Add the garlic, spices and salt and cook for five minutes, stirring continuously.

Add the tomato purée and simmer gently for 15 minutes.

PER SERVING:
279 Calories
5g Carbs
40g Protein
11g Fat

72 DINNER

Fragrant mince

1 large red onion, finely sliced
400g extra lean beef mince/low fat Quorn mince*
2 tbsps curry powder
150g red lentils (dry weight)
700ml chicken or vegetable stock (see recipes on page 35)
1 x 200g can chopped tomatoes
2-3 tomatoes
handful coriander leaves
50g per person uncooked basmati rice

SERVES 4

** **Note:** Some meat free alternatives contain gluten and/or MSG. Please check the label before you buy!*

In a non-stick frying pan, dry-fry the onion and mince over a high heat for two minutes, breaking up the mince as you go.

Stir in the curry powder and lentils. Pour in stock and bring to a gentle boil, then simmer for 10-15 minutes. Add the tinned tomatoes.

While the mince is cooking, dice the tomatoes and roughly chop the coriander, then mix together in a small bowl.

Place the rice in a large saucepan of cold salted water and bring to the boil. Simmer gently until cooked and drain well.

Serve the mince on a bed of rice, with a few spoonfuls of the tomato and coriander salad.

PER SERVING:
485 Calories
62g Carbs
39g Protein
9g Fat

Ryan-Lindsey-Fitness | 07547 192913   DINNER

Spicy yam soup

2 tbsps olive oil
500g turkey steaks, diced/Quorn meat free chicken*
400g yam, peeled and cubed
1 cauliflower head, cut into large florets
1 x 400ml can light unsweetened coconut milk
200ml cold fresh water
1 x 400g can cannellini beans, drained and rinsed
1 tsp chilli flakes
1 large sprig chopped fresh basil
1 tbsp soy sauce
1 tsp dry mustard powder
1 tsp ground coriander
1 tsp paprika
½ tsp ground ginger
½ tsp ground cardamom
½ tsp ground turmeric
1 bay leaf
1 cinnamon stick
salt and pepper
1 large sprig chopped fresh parsley

SERVES 4

PER SERVING:
498 Calories
38g Carbs
46g Protein
18g Fat

__Note:__ Some meat free alternatives contain gluten and/or MSG. Please check the label before you buy!

Heat the oil in a large skillet over a medium heat. Cook the turkey/Quorn meat free chicken for 5 minutes, turning to brown all over. Add the yams and cook for around 8 minutes, stirring regularly until fork-tender.

Add the cauliflower and continue cooking for 10 minutes.

Combine the coconut milk, water, and cannellini beans in a large saucepan over a medium/high heat.

Stir the chilli flakes, basil, soy sauce, mustard powder, coriander, paprika, ground ginger, cardamom, turmeric, bay leaf and cinnamon stick into the bean mixture. Add more water if needed.

Season the soup with salt and black pepper. Bring to the boil, add the yam mixture and reduce heat to a low temperature. Simmer for 45 minutes. Spoon into bowls, garnished with parsley.

74 DINNER

Spicy Thai burgers

For the burgers:
450g lean turkey mince/low fat Quorn mince*
1 medium sized egg
20g fresh coriander, finely chopped, plus extra to garnish
1 green chilli, finely sliced
2 spring onions, finely sliced
1 tsp Thai 7 Spice seasoning
half a small red onion, peeled and finely chopped
slice of fresh lime to garnish

For the vegetable side dishes:
2 large sweet potatoes
1 tsp ground cinnamon
10 cherry tomatoes, sliced in half
50g baby leaf spinach

MAKES 5 BURGERS AND 3 SERVINGS OF MASH AND VEG

Note: Some meat free alternatives contain gluten and/or MSG. Please check the label before you buy!

Preheat oven to 175°C.

In a large bowl, mash up the mince, using a masher or your hands. Add the remaining burger ingredients and mix well until well combined. Shape the mixture into 5 patties, then transfer to a lightly greased baking tray. Oven cook for 10 minutes. Turn over and cook for a 10-15 minutes. The juices will run clear when cooked.

For the vegetable side dishes:
Bake the sweet potatoes in the oven for 45 minutes or until soft. Using a fork, scrape the contents of the potatoes into a bowl. Discard the skin. Mash thoroughly and season well. Stir in the cinnamon.

Pour cold water into a non-stick frying pan (just enough to cover the base). Add the tomatoes and cook gently for 2 minutes, stirring frequently. Add the spinach and wilt gently.

The burgers and mash can both be kept in the fridge for up to 3 days.

PER BURGER / VEG SIDE DISHES:
154 Calories / 156 Calories
1g Carbs / 35g Carbs
33g Protein / 4g Protein
2g Fat / 0g Fat

Ryan-Lindsey-Fitness | 07547 192913

Satay spice kebabs

IDEAL FOR BBQ

juice of one medium sized orange
2 tsps orange zest
2 tbsps peanut butter
3 tbsps soy sauce
1 inch piece ginger, peeled and finely chopped
4 garlic cloves, minced
1 tsp acacia honey
2 tsp red chilli flakes
450g chicken breast/Quorn meat free chicken*, diced
pre-soaked wooden skewers

SERVES 3

Note: Some meat free alternatives contain gluten and/or MSG. Please check the label before you buy!

Mix together the orange juice, orange zest, peanut butter, soy sauce, ginger, garlic, honey and red chilli flakes until the mixture is smooth.

Stir in the chicken, ensuring it is evenly coated. Refrigerate for at least 30 minutes (maximum of 8 hours).

Preheat oven to 150°C and, if using a barbecue, prepare it for cooking.

Remove the chicken from the marinade and discard marinade ingredients. Cook chicken in the oven for 20 minutes, then turn and cook for a further 25 minutes.

Finish on the barbecue for 20 minutes (or continue to cook in the oven).

Serve with a crispy salad.

PER SERVING:
344 Calories
11g **Carbs**
48g **Protein**
12g **Fat**

Lime chicken fajitas

IDEAL FOR BBQ

500g chicken breast/Quorn meat free chicken*, diced
juice of 2 limes
4 cloves garlic, finely chopped
1 tbsp olive oil
1 red pepper, sliced
1 green pepper, sliced
1 yellow pepper, sliced
1 medium sized white onion, finely sliced
½ tsp ground cumin
¼ tsp salt
¼ tsp ground black pepper
pre-soaked wooden skewers

SERVES 3

Note: Some meat free alternatives contain gluten and/or MSG. Please check the label before you buy!

Preheat the oven to 150°C, or alternatively, prepare the barbecue for cooking.

Put the chicken in a bowl. Combine the lime juice and about half of the garlic. Pour the mixture over the chicken, coating thoroughly. Cover the dish and allow it to marinate in the refrigerator for 30 minutes.

PER SERVING:
325 Calories
12g Carbs
49g Protein
9g Fat

Avoid leaving the chicken to marinate for too long, as the lime juice will break down too much of the tissue.

Remove from fridge and thread several chicken pieces onto each skewer. Place the chicken on the barbecue or in the oven and turn regularly until cooked through (around 20 minutes).

Heat the oil in a large skillet over a medium heat. Add the peppers, onion and remaining garlic to the skillet. Cook for around five minutes or until tender, stirring regularly. Sprinkle with cumin, salt and pepper.

Serve the fajita mix topped with the chicken, with a side salad.

Ryan-Lindsey-Fitness | 07547 192913

RyanLindseyFitness
Be so good they can't ignore you

Made in the USA
Charleston, SC
04 May 2015